MARQUIS DE LAFAYETTE

The Hero of Two Worlds Biography 4th Grade Children's Biography Books

The Marquis de Lafayette was a member of the French nobility, but he fought hard for the rights of the common people. Find out about his life both in France and in America!

BORN TO WEALTH

The Marquis de Lafayette's full name was Marie-Joseph Paul Yves Roche Gilbert du Motier. He was born in 1757. By the time he was twelve, both his mother and father had died and he had inherited a great estate and the title of marquis.

The Château de Chavaniac

Marquis de Lafayette statue

In 1771, at fourteen, Lafayette joined the French army and trained as an officer. When he married at 16, he became a part of the king's extended family.

PASSION FOR LIBERTY

Lafayette was aware from an early age of the great difficulties in France, where a small number of nobles owned most of the money and held most of the power in the country, while the great majority of the people suffered. He could not see how to work to change things in France, but in 1775 he started to learn about the struggles of the English settlers in America.

Portrait of Lafayette

Marquis de Lafayette

The Duke of Gloucester, brother of the King of England, painted a romantic, sympathetic picture of the colonists trying to get fairer treatment from the government in London. Lafayette determined to go to America to see if he could help.

Helping ordinary people struggle against their king was not normally something any king would approve of, so Lafayette had to sneak out of France and cross the Atlantic without permission from the French king.

Lafayette and Washington

A YOUNG GENERAL

By the time Lafayette arrived in America in 1777, the American colonies had declared their independence and were at war with England. The Americans welcomed Lafayette happily. He was not much of a military force, since he was not even twenty years old and had never yet been in a battle, but he symbolized France's support for the independence efforts. Some American leaders also hoped Lafayette could convince France to send troops to help in the war.

The Continental Congress gave Lafayette the rank of Major General and assigned him to the staff of General George Washington. He participated in the Battle of the Brandywine in September, 1777, and was wounded in the leg. Despite being shot he was able to organize a successful retreat for his forces.

Battle of Brandywine

When he recovered, Lafayette joined the army in winter quarters. There, he learned of some officers who were trying to get General Washington replaced. Lafayette wrote strong letters in support of Washington and helped frustrate the plan to replace him.

General Gates was head of the Board of War. He wanted to take control of the war away from General Washington. He came up with a plan to invade the British territories in what is now Canada, and ordered Lafayette to go to Albany to take part in the expedition. Gates hoped success in this attack would increase his power and lower Washington's standing.

General Gates

Lafayette statue at Mount Vernon

In Albany, Lafayette found that there were serious problems with the planned invasion. There were not enough troops, and they did not have enough supplies. The commanding generals were sure the attack would fail, if for no other reason, because the British knew of the plans and were already prepared to meet and defeat the Americans.

Lafayette wrote a detailed report of the situation to the Continental Congress, pointing out that the plan had a great chance of failure. Based in large part on Lafayette's report, the Americans cancelled their invasion plans.

Lafayette took part in the American efforts in 1778 to capture Newport, Rhode Island, a strong British base. The British brought in more and more troops, and the American forces withdrew in some confusion. Lafayette took command of the rearguard, the forces closest to the British lines, and helped more than a thousand American soldiers escape from being captured or shot.

GETTING HELP IN FRANCE

At the end of the fighting season in 1778, Lafayette went back to France on leave. He made his apologies to the king for going to America without permission, and reunited with his wife and family.

Lafayette worked hard to convince France to send money, supplies, warships and troops to aid the Americans. He pointed out to some people the importance of supporting human rights and the struggle for freedom. To others, like the king, he talked more about how helping the Americans would weaken the English, France's long-time enemy.

In 1780 Lafayette was able to report that France had agreed to provide military support to the Americans in their rebellion. He also spent large sums of his own money to buy supplies for the American troops.

Marie-Joseph Paul Yves Roche Gilbert du Motier

Siege of Yorktown

BACK IN AMERICA

The French support Lafayette had arranged was essential in helping defeat the British armies. The last great battle of the Revolutionary War happened at Yorktown, Virginia in 1781. The American army, with French troops and cannons in support, kept the British from leaving Yorktown by land, and the French fleet kept the British from getting away by sea. Lafayette commanded some of the land forces. With the loss of that army, the British moved toward ending their war with the new nation of the United States.

WORKING FOR REFORM IN FRANCE

Back in France, Lafayette became a strong supporter of the effort to reform the French government and French society. He was a member of the gathering at Versailles in 1789 that met to correct some wrongs that were damaging France, and which marked the start of the French Revolution.

Versailles

DÉCLARATION DES DROITS DE L'HOMME ET DU CITOYEN

Décrétés par l'Assemblée Nationale dans les séances des 20, 21, 23, 24 et 26 août 1789, acceptés par le Roi

PRÉAMBULE

LES représentans du peuple François, constitués en assemblée nationale, considérant que l'ignorance, l'oubli ou le mépris des droits de l'homme sont les seules causes des malheurs publics et de la corruption des gouvernemens, ont résolu d'exposer dans une déclaration solemnelle, les droits naturels, inaliénables et sacrés de l'homme, afin que cette déclaration, constamment présente à tous les membres du corps social, leur rappelle sans cesse leurs droits et leurs devoirs; afin que les actes du pouvoir législatif et ceux du pouvoir exécutif, pouvant être à chaque instant comparés avec le but de toute institution politique, en soient plus respectés; afin que les réclamations des citoyens, fondées désormais sur des principes simples et incontestables, tournent toujours au maintien de la constitution et du bonheur de tous.

EN conséquence, l'assemblée nationale reconnoit et déclare, en présence et sous les auspices de l'Etre suprême les droits suivans de l'homme et du citoyen.

ARTICLE PREMIER
LES hommes naissent et demeurent libres et égaux en droits; les distinctions sociales ne peuvent être fondées que sur l'utilité commune.

II.
LE but de toute association politique est la conservation des droits naturels et imprescriptibles de l'homme; ces droits sont la liberté, la propriété, la sûreté, et la résistance à l'oppression.

III.
LE principe de toute souveraineté réside essentiellement dans la nation; nul corps, nul individu ne peut exercer d'autorité qui n'en émane expressément.

IV.
LA liberté consiste à pouvoir faire tout ce qui ne nuit pas à autrui. Ainsi, l'exercice des droits naturels de chaque homme, n'a de bornes que celles qui assurent aux autres membres de la société la jouissance de ces mêmes droits; ces bornes ne peuvent être déterminées que par la loi.

V.
LA loi n'a le droit de défendre que les actions nuisibles à la société. Tout ce qui n'est pas défendu par la loi ne peut être empêché, et nul ne peut être contraint à faire ce qu'elle n'ordonne pas.

VI.
LA loi est l'expression de la volonté générale: tous les citoyens ont droit de concourir personnellement, ou par leurs représentans, à sa formation; elle doit être la même pour tous, soit qu'elle protège, soit qu'elle punisse. Tous les citoyens étant égaux à ses yeux, sont également admissibles à toutes dignités, places et emplois publics, selon leur capacité, et sans autres distinction que celles de leurs vertus et de leurs talens.

VII.
NUL homme ne peut être accusé, arrêté ni détenu que dans les cas déterminés par la loi, et selon les formes qu'elle a prescrites; ceux qui sollicitent, expédient, exécutent ou font exécuter des ordres arbitraires, doivent être punis; mais tout citoyen appelé ou saisi en vertu de la loi, doit obéir à l'instant; il se rend coupable par la résistance.

VIII.
LA loi ne doit établir que des peines strictement et évidemment nécessaire, et nul ne peut être puni qu'en vertu d'une loi établie et promulguée antérieurement au délit, et légalement appliquée.

IX.
TOUT homme étant présumé innocent jusqu'à ce qu'il ait été déclaré coupable, s'il est jugé indispensable de l'arrêter, toute rigueur qui ne serait pas nécessaire pour s'assurer de sa personne doit être sévèrement réprimée par la loi.

X.
NUL ne doit être inquiété pour ses opinions, mêmes religieuses, pourvu que leur manifestation ne trouble pas l'ordre public établi par la loi.

XI.
LA libre communication des pensées et des opinions est un des droits les plus précieux de l'homme: tout citoyen peut donc parler, écrire, imprimer librement: sauf à répondre de l'abus de cette liberté dans les cas déterminés par la loi.

XII.
LA garantie des droits de l'homme et du citoyen nécessite une force publique; cette force est donc instituée pour l'avantage de tous, et non pour l'utilité particulière de ceux à qui elle est confiée.

XIII.
POUR l'entretien de la force publique, et pour les dépenses d'administration, une contribution commune est indispensable; elle doit être également répartie entre les citoyens en raison de leurs facultés.

XIV.
LES citoyens ont le droit de constater par eux même ou par leurs représentans, la nécessité de la contribution publique, de la consentir librement, d'en suivre l'emploi, et d'en déterminer la quotité, l'assiette, le recouvrement et la durée.

XV.
LA société a le droit de demander compte à tout agent public de son administration.

XVI.
TOUTE société, dans laquelle la garantie des droits n'est pas assurée, ni la séparation des pouvoirs déterminée, n'a point de constitution.

XVII.
LES propriétés étant un droit inviolable et sacré, nul ne peut en être privé, si ce n'est lorsque la nécessité publique, légalement constatée, l'exige évidemment, et sous la condition d'une juste et préalable indemnité.

AUX REPRESENTANS DU PEUPLE FRANCOIS

Lafayette was a co-author of an important document, the "Declaration of the Rights of Man and of the Citizen". The declaration laid out universal rights, including the rights to freedom of thought, speech, assembly, and worship, and to equal treatment under the law, that we take for granted now but which were radical ideas in the eighteenth century. The National Assembly adopted the declaration in 1789, and it is still part of France's constitution today.

Lafayette was commander of the National Guard. In 1789, when a huge mob marched on Versailles to force the king to move to Paris and to respond to their demands, Lafayette played a major part in keeping violence to a minimum. Read the Baby Professor book, Moms Needed Bread!, to learn more about that march.

Lafayette as commander of the National Guard

French Revolution

DANGER

Lafayette was very popular and was a friend to the efforts of the French Revolution to make a fairer and more just country. But to the more radical leaders of the Revolution, he was an enemy just because he was a member of the nobility.

Lafayette realized he might be arrested and executed at any time, so he fled France in 1792. He was captured by Austria, which was at war with France, and held a prisoner by Austria and Prussia until 1797.

Napoleon Bonaparte

Finally, Napoleon Bonaparte, who was on the edge of making himself the sole ruler of France, got Lafayette released and he was able to return to France in 1800. Lafayette came home to find his wealth gone and his properties ruined.

LATER YEARS

Lafayette turned down important political offices over the next years, concentrating on restoring and managing his property at La Grange, near Paris. He had spent huge amounts of his own money to support the American Revolution, and eventually the US Congress sent him $200,000 as a partial repayment. Later Congress granted him land in the new territory of Louisiana.

La Grange

Lafayette at laying of corner stone

When Lafayette visited the United States in 1824, his tour was like that of a modern rock star. Huge crowds turned out to see him. He laid the cornerstone of the famous war monument at Bunker Hill, near Boston.

In 1830, France's King Charles X dissolved the National Assembly and took other actions to restore the power of the king. Lafayette, at the age of 72, took command of the National Guard and marched to Paris to support those opposed to the king.

Charles X

The Oath of Lafayette at the
Festival of the Federation, 14 July 1790

After the king was forced from the throne, people asked Lafayette to become dictator of France, but he turned down the offer.

Lafayette died in 1834, at age 77. He was buried in a Paris cemetery next to his wife. His son covered the coffin with dirt they had brought back from the Bunker Hill battlefield in 1825, to honor Lafayette's request to be buried in both French and American soil.

Grave of the Marquis de Lafayette

Until the end of his life, Lafayette was a strong and active champion of the rights of common people on both sides of the Atlantic Ocean. He also had other influences on American life: he made a gift of seven large dogs to General Washington. The dogs, bred with English Foxhounds, were the parents of a new and popular dog breed, the American Foxhound.

DANGEROUS, EXCITING TIMES

The years from the start of the American Revolution in 1776 to the end of the French Revolution in 1798 were full of excitement, danger, high intentions and low deeds. Find out more about the French Revolution in Baby Professor books like *Are You With Us or Against Us? Looking Back on the Reign of Terror* and *The French Revolution: People Power in Action* to learn even more.

Battle of Arcole (1796)

Visit

BABY PROFESSOR
EDUCATION KIDS

www.BabyProfessorBooks.com
to download Free Baby Professor eBooks
and view our catalog of new and exciting
Children's Books

www.ingramcontent.com/pod-product-compliance
Lightning Source LLC
Chambersburg PA
CBHW081959160726
47999CB00008B/2672